The Heart of Leadership

A Personal Reflection

Dr. LaVerne Harmon

 Published in 2019 by Dr. LaVerne Harmon.

www.theheartofleadership.org

Harmon, LaVerne, Dr., author

The Heart of Leadership / Dr. LaVerne Harmon.

Issued in print and electronic formats.

ISBN 978-0-578-54250-8

Printed in the United States of America

ISBN 978-0-578-54250-8

Dedicated to

all the people who have

touched my heart.

Table of Contents

Preface

The Heart of Leadership is written to edify professionals about a powerful force that drives the actions and behaviors of many successful and respected leaders: compassion. My observations and experiences have shown that when compassion is part of every interaction and decision, there is usually a decline in personnel issues, conflicts and many more distractions that take valuable time away from accomplishing goals. My sole purpose for writing this book is to share what I've learned about leadership based on the experiences I've had during my career. If you wish to lead, I encourage you to take an inventory of your treatment of others — and a hard look at yourself. You may become aware of any adverse behaviors and make an effort to improve your leadership capability.

I sincerely hope that what I've written will inspire you to be mindful of your treatment of others. Believe it or not, my first draft was written many years before this book was actually published. I've read it, reread it, and edited it many times while wondering if it would be useful to anyone. I present it to you with humility and love.

As you read this book, you'll learn how to incorporate compassion into your daily life and experience serenity like never before while instilling positive energy into the lives of others.

Keep in mind that life is a series of lessons that mold and change us—hopefully into better human beings and productive citizens. I'm not the same person I was 20 years ago, and I'm not the same person I was last year. Every experience teaches us something new, and my experiences taught me a lot! For better or worse, I wouldn't change a thing.

Dr LaVerne Harmon

THE HEART OF LEADERSHIP – A PERSONAL REFLECTION

Introduction

"Leadership is not so much about technique and methods as it is about opening the heart. Leadership is about inspiration of oneself and of others. Great leadership is about human experiences, not processes. Leadership is not a formula or a program, it is a human activity that comes from the heart and considers the heart of others. It is an attitude, not a routine."

~Dr. Lance Secretan, Industry Week

Introduction

Experience is often the best teacher. Whether perceived as good or bad, experiences are necessary for intellectual and spiritual growth. Once you grasp this concept, you begin to look for the lesson in each experience and learn to endure—and to be thankful—no matter what blocks your path. You realize there's no need to complain, condemn, resent, become negative or hold a grudge.

Without the experiences that have occurred in my life, I would not have gained the wisdom and knowledge to write this book and share what I believe is the most important characteristic of leadership. The only sources used while putting this guide together were my personal experiences, intuitive sense, inherent insight, and inspiration from God.

Despite what some might think, leadership is not complicated. Various leadership styles and techniques are explained in textbooks and taught in classrooms, seminars, webinars and lectures. However, the core of good leadership lies within the individual. So many times intelligent leaders fail because they lack self-control. They don't understand themselves or others. They rule by intimidation. They abuse their power.

In addition to intelligence and vision, the many qualities needed for successful leadership include selflessness, insightfulness, composure, humility, and most important, compassion. Have we placed so much emphasis on research and theory that we've forgotten about love, the greatest, most important common element within each of us? Love is at the heart of compassion. Knowledge is essential, but knowledge without compassion could be disastrous in decision-making and other leadership situations. We avoid mistakes by having compassion. It should form the foundation for everything we do.

A compassionate leadership style will earn you respect and help you build a dedicated, loyal and hardworking team. If you adapt compassion and practice it daily in the workplace, your employees' confidence and productivity levels will increase. Groups or teams will become more cohesive and supportive of one another. Leaders within your group will emerge. Employees, even very experienced ones, will be more receptive to change. You'll hear things like, "I love my job," or, "I really enjoy coming to work every day," or "I had a wonderful vacation, but I missed being at work."

The many hours we spend on the job distance us from our families and other interests. Time, one of our most valuable resources, is often taken for granted. Human beings are our most precious resources and they are sometimes overlooked, mistreated and unappreciated. What a waste of time and talent! Don't you think we should start paying more attention to creating a productive, pleasant and stress-free environment? I've heard about too many people who are miserable and dread going to work every day. Life is meant to be enjoyed — even at work.

The things we do and the decisions we make as leaders can have a positive or negative impact on others. I choose to make a positive impact and hope you will, too. As you read this book, be mindful of the mistakes you've made and begin to make a conscious effort to include compassion in your daily leadership duties. Compassion is at the root of every idea discussed in this text. If practiced, you'll become more tolerant, understanding, gracious, considerate, more respected and less stressed — and you'll be a more effective leader.

What is Compassion?

"I would rather feel compassion than know the meaning of it."

~Thomas Aquinas

What is Compassion?

In my experience, having compassion allows you to be kind and considerate of the feelings and welfare of others. A compassionate person is more likely to be patient, caring and unselfish. Some may view compassion as a weakness, but it's quite the opposite. With genuine compassion, it's possible to have power over your emotions, attitude and actions, and to rise above adverse situations. It takes more strength and courage to respond with kindness in situations of conflict, crisis, insubordination and confusion. You can't prevent confrontations or controversies, but having compassion helps you to manage your reactions to them.

Try to apply the Thomas Aquinas quote that started this chapter to leaders and leadership. To me, it means that there's not much benefit in understanding the definition of compassion if you don't practice or feel it. Practicing compassion requires you to make a conscious change in behavior and develop a genuine desire to change. Being aware of your actions and focusing on doing the right thing will come naturally. Nobody's perfect, so understand that you will make mistakes, become annoyed, act too hastily without getting the facts, or react negatively in the heat of conflict. But if you consistently practice compassion, you can minimize and avoid these occurrences and change negative behaviors. It will stimulate the positive behavior required of successful leadership. When you feel compassion, you'll apologize when you've offended or falsely accused someone. You'll praise others, including people who have more expertise in certain areas than you do. You'll be concerned about the welfare of those you supervise and even those you don't.

Don't misunderstand: Compassion doesn't mean you don't hold others accountable. Of course you do! But there's a way to do that by setting expectations, providing the resources and development needed to be successful. If the employee's follow-through is less than acceptable, the situation needs to be evaluated. In some instances, tough decisions have to be made.

Lead with love. It's not enough to know the meaning of compassion; you must feel it in your heart and practice it every day.

Why is compassion so important?

"Not all people lead with compassion, but those who do are more effective."

~Dr. LaVerne Harmon

Why is Compassion So Important?

As beneficial as compassion is in leadership, it's surprisingly rare in the workplace. I compare it to a cardinal showing up in the middle of a snowstorm. It doesn't happen very often, but when it does, everyone in view notices it. The same is true in the professional world. Not all people lead with compassion, but those who do are more effective. A compassionate leader will be noticed for his or her patience and understanding.

When you practice compassion, you have to be aware of your inappropriate conduct. You learn to recognize when you're being unfair, or exhibiting other negative behaviors. When you pay attention to your feelings, a silent, inner voice lets you know when you're off course and not functioning with compassion. Listen to it.

People are hurt on a daily basis because they're forced to deal with self-serving leaders. There are negative leaders who create toxic working environments that affect everyone around them. He or she is the kind of leader who causes unpleasant working conditions that could inspire poor morale and decreased productivity levels.

The following sections offer insight into how leaders can create pleasant and productive work environments.

Wise Decision-making and Good Judgment

"Gaining understanding and acceptance of your views and decisions should be your motivation and goal when presenting new directions and organizational changes."

~Dr. LaVerne Harmon

Wise Decision-Making and Good Judgment

When confronted with situations, conflicts or personnel issues, take time before making decisions to reflect on potential consequences. Poor judgment is often due to hasty reactions and conclusions. That's not just the easy way out; it can also be costly. Remember to gather facts and details so that you'll have a frame of reference from which to draw conclusions. Ask questions, discuss concerns, and listen to what others have to say. This is not the time to be impulsive. Analyze situations critically before making decisions. Always keep in mind that people will be affected by your decisions. Their welfare should be your concern.

When you write a dissertation or research paper, you end with conclusions. Before the conclusion, an issue or problem is identified, data is gathered, relevant history is reviewed and findings are reported. Conclusions are based on evidence that either supports or rejects the hypothesis. With that research, improvements have been made, solutions have been discovered, and mistakes have been avoided.

When struggling with difficult situations, using this form of in-depth analysis is excellent, but when you combine it with compassion, you can make intelligent decisions.

Objectivity is another important element of wise decision-making and good judgment. I can't stress enough the importance of being objective. It's critical to remove all personal biases and preconceptions that could interfere with your ability to use sound judgment or make sensible, impartial decisions. Objective reasoning will earn you the reputation of being fair.

Strong, confident leaders are not afraid to make unpopular decisions. Many times, leaders will stay in the middle of the road on issues, fearing what will happen if they go left or right. Be fearless. The middle of the road is a dangerous place to be; it's an accident waiting to happen.

Leaders have to be willing to stand up and make those hard, sometimes unpopular decisions. Know where you stand and be prepared to stand up for what you believe. Stay in the middle of the road and you'll hinder progress. Everything will be at a standstill; there will be no way around you. Move confidently in one direction. Good judgment and compassion will help you decide how to navigate the path.

Your choice of direction should be articulated in detail, and in a manner that's positive, clear and supportive of the organization as a whole. Even though everyone involved may not agree with your decision, you'll be respected and viewed as a strong leader. There will be a greater chance that others will change direction and follow you. Most of the time, open, honest communication is all it takes to get everyone on board. Gaining understanding and acceptance of your views and decisions should be your motivation and goal when presenting new directions and organizational changes.

Make a decision and live with it regardless of how unpopular it might be. You can't worry about those who won't like you. You will never please everyone. If your heart is in the right place, it's easier to make a tough decision knowing your only consideration is what's best for the organization. Make the best decision you can with the information you have and move forward with compassion.

Assumptions, Accusations and Speculations

"Erroneous assumptions can be disastrous."

~Peter Drucker

Assumptions, Accusations and Speculations

ne of the worst things a leader can do that cause him or her to lose respect is to accuse someone wrongly, or to make accusations based on assumptions. Making false accusations causes anger and frustration. If you do this, be quick to apologize sincerely.

Speculation is a waste of time and energy. It's a guessing game that doesn't solve anything. Instead of escalating a situation with "what if," or " I suppose," or "I think," wait until you know the facts. Speculation can cause overreaction. You exacerbate a situation by reacting to what you think has occurred. This behavior also creates negative emotions and clouds judgment. It puts you in a place where compassion cannot reside.

Maintain your composure when things around you appear chaotic. Wait until you have more information about a situation to avoid making assumptions and poor decisions that are based on speculation.

Gossip

"I resolve to speak ill of no man whatever, not even in a matter of truth; but rather by some means excuse the faults I hear charged upon others, and upon proper occasions speak all the good I know of everybody."

~Benjamin Franklin

Gossip

I refer to gossip as a deadly weapon you don't want to be charged with possessing. Gossip has the power to destroy. It can ruin relationships, tarnish reputations, turn people against each other and distract them from the goals of an organization.

Know your staff; those you can trust and those you can't. Know the difference between gossip and essential information that could be damaging to the department or organization. Pay attention to people who bring you information. You can discern whether it's based on concern or backstabbing. Don't allow one employee to bring negative information to you that's damaging to another's reputation. If this occurs, take advantage of the opportunity to turn a negative remark or comment into a positive one. Offer a comment expressing something good about the individual or doubt about the subject. The worst thing you can do is feed into negativity. Contributing to gossip adds fuel to it. And it will spread like wildfire.

If, however, information brought to you is vital, and the person delivering it is trustworthy, pay attention. You can't always know, but with compassion, your view of the information will be focused on care and concern for all involved parties. In time you'll be able to discern who has your best interests at heart and who is out to gossip and hurt someone.

One of the ways to stop gossip is to make it clear that you won't tolerate this kind of behavior, and that all parties involved will be engaged in an open discussion. This practice creates a culture grounded in trust. Remember, potentially harmful remarks or conversations about an individual should not be entertained without the person present to defend him- or herself.

Praise and Recognition

"There is something that is much more scarce, something rarer than ability. It is the ability to recognize ability."

~Robert Half

Praise and Recognition

Great leaders bring out the best in others. Encourage others through praise. Recognize the talents and accomplishments of individuals and let them know you value their contributions. Praise boosts self-confidence and self-esteem, and increases productivity levels. Recognize strengths and positive attributes. Strive to make employees feel good about themselves.

Celebrate accomplishments; it's good for morale. Build a reputation of being a person who gives credit where credit is due. Acknowledge others for their ideas and creativity. If someone expresses a great idea, don't turn it around and make it your own. Too many times I've witnessed a leader take someone's suggestion, recommendation or innovative idea, and present it as his or her own without giving recognition. This type of behavior can cause creative people to shut down. Leaders have to remember that it's not about them; it's about the organization. When you lead with compassion, you value and acknowledge the ideas of others.

Remember to recognize the role each person plays in the successful completion of a goal or task. It's amazing how a small compliment will motivate and encourage workers to do even more. And, it creates a positive working environment. John Quincy Adams understood the critical role leaders play in encouraging others. He said, "If your actions inspire others to dream more, learn more, do more and become more, you are a leader."

Criticism

"He has a right to criticize who has a heart to help."

~Abraham Lincoln

Criticism

Criticism should always be presented in a careful, constructive and professional manner so that it promotes growth and development. When employees know what they're doing wrong, they're more inclined to be receptive to criticism. They perceive that the leader genuinely wants them to be successful. Suggest ways to improve and strengthen weaknesses. Encourage employees to advance their training and education so they can reach their full potential. Never use an individual's weaknesses to set them up for failure. If the employee is hardworking and loyal, every effort should be made to find a position that matches his or her strengths. Take time to talk with your staff about their goals and career aspirations and offer advice to help achieve them.

Criticizing staff members publicly is humiliating and hurtful. Employees may lose respect for you. When you criticize an employee constantly, he or she can shut down and stop offering input during discussions or meetings. Everyone's opinions and feelings matter, but when people fear criticism, they keep their great ideas or solutions to themselves. They stop speaking out.

Use constructive criticism to teach and boost self-esteem. Add a little compassion and practice patience when dealing with peoples' shortcomings. We all have them. Recognize them in yourself, and you'll be ahead of the game.

Team Building

"The leaders who work most effectively, it seems to me, never say "I." And that's not because ... they trained themselves not to say "I." They don't think "I." They think "we"; they think "team." They accept responsibility and don't sidestep it, but "we" gets the credit. This is what creates trust, what enables you to get the task done."

~Peter Drucker

Team Building

Building a cohesive team begins with servant leaders who support each other and operate in a unified, respectful manner. In other words, leaders must set an example if they want other members of the organization to function as a team. Work together, not in isolation, to accomplish goals. Be willing to help a colleague in a tough situation by being supportive and involved in the process. Compassionate leaders will not operate territorially. They understand that completing goals successfully is more important than who gets the credit.

Leaders can empower staff by including them in the decision-making process. This gives them ownership in the task and reinforces the team concept. Demonstrate to employees how their input is valued and helps create success. Build and promote an environment that's supportive of the organization's mission. Teach employees that no department stands alone and the needs of the organization have to be considered and prioritized. As a leader, even if you don't agree with decisions of the executive team, express support anyway, particularly when communicating changes and new policies and procedures to employees. It promotes unity across all company lines, thus encouraging the team concept organization-wide.

Methods, techniques and concepts for building a cohesive team are embedded within each section of this book. Compassion in leadership is the most powerful tool for developing an effective team that works together with respect, kindness and passion. Remember, stability in a department requires a leader who is compassionate, understanding and knowledgeable. Without those attributes, the team can fall apart. Productivity and morale can drop, and when that happens, leaders can lose respect.

Reprimand and Discipline

"A ruler should be slow to punish and swift to reward."

~Ovid

Reprimand and Discipline

Life is a series of lessons. The toughest and best lessons are learned from our own mistakes, and we've all made them. We learn in every situation, and the working environment is no exception. Allow for mistakes. Don't expect perfection. Set policies and procedures to avoid repeating the same mistakes. If reprimand or discipline is warranted, make sure it's fair, appropriate, and done in a manner that's respectful and preserves a person's dignity.

Use your authority to empower, not overpower. Scare tactics are counterproductive and lower morale. Threats, especially of being fired, don't solve anything. They cause anxiety, worry and fear, and all of that interferes with an individual's performance. In many cases, it makes the situation worse by creating an atmosphere of defensiveness, paranoia and chaos. If this is the only way you can get others to work on your behalf, I believe something is lacking in your leadership style. Good leaders can influence and motivate others without using force. Intimidation will not gain respect. Leaders must give respect to get respect. It recalls a famous line from the film, "Mutiny on the Bounty:" "Bring men to duty by lifting their hearts, not by tyranny, hatred or cruelty."

Share Knowledge and Experiences

"The growth and development of people is the highest calling of leadership."

Harvey S. Firestone

Share Knowledge and Experiences

Share your knowledge, experiences and lessons you've learned with your subordinates. Imparting experiences is one of the best ways for others to learn what to do and not to do. It's a great opportunity to contribute to the growth, development, knowledge and success of future leaders. Wisdom and knowledge are gained through experience, so why not talk about your career path, your experiences as a leader, the bumps in the road, and how you overcame them? Discuss tough decisions you made, the results of those decisions, and what you learned from those results.

Leaders become teachers to those who truly listen. They hear what they say and watch what they do. A compassionate leader has a desire to want others to be better prepared and more equipped than they are, especially those who have leadership potential or have been identified as future leaders. Being a mentor and motivator will help instill pride and confidence in others. Use your life lessons to pave the bumpy roads those future leaders will have to follow.

Are you secure enough as a leader to prepare future leaders to be more successful than you? If you lead with compassion, the answer will be YES!

Power

"Nearly all men can stand adversity, but if you want to test a man's character, give him power."

~Abraham Lincoln

Power

Titles are only words. They don't define who you are. They simply clarify your rank and sometimes offer positional power. My advice is never to let the power of your position go to your head, and never use it to mistreat others. Avoid being cruel and unjust. Would you rather be known as the one in charge or the respected leader with whom everyone wants to work? Mohandas Gandhi said: "Learn to use respect to win people over and convince them to follow you with their hearts, instead of using your power to bend people to your will."

A tyrant can have a title of vice president or president, and if they use power because of a title, they're not respected. Compassionate leaders are humble human beings who let their moral compass guide them. That's real power!

Don't walk around with an air of superiority. Make a conscious effort to greet and acknowledge everyone. Remember their names and specific accomplishments so you can address them personally while adding a positive comment about their contributions. Give all employees equal recognition and respect— regardless of their positions.

We all have unique gifts and talents. Know your strengths and weaknesses and don't compare yourself to others. Forget about being in control of your personal agenda, and then focus on accomplishing what's best for the organization. Be secure enough to surround yourself with experts in areas where you are not as strong, then credit them for the value they add.

I've witnessed insecure leaders intentionally demean or stifle subordinates who were more talented in certain areas. That's not compassion. A compassionate leader would utilize the talents of all employees, regardless of their positions.

It's not about you! Abusing power affects your ability to lead successfully. Take the focus off of you and pay attention to the needs of your staff. Confident leaders don't look for rewards or praise; insecure leaders do.

Greater are the rewards when the focus is placed on the needs and successes of those around you. Jealousy and resentment have no place in a leader's heart.

Can you honestly say you've been sincerely happy for someone's success, promotion or good fortune? If you can't, ask yourself why. Is it jealousy or resentment? Is it a lack of compassion and care for others? My advice to you is to look within yourself and make a concerted effort to change. Compassionate leaders constantly examine these things within themselves.

Communication

"The greatest motivational act one person can do for another is listen."

~Robert E. Moody

Communication

Frequent communication can prevent a host of issues and problems. Meet regularly with your staff. Listen to their concerns and suggestions. Include everyone in the group during conversations. Make everyone feel that their input is valued and their opinions respected. This creates an atmosphere of open communication. You will be perceived as a good listener and employees will be comfortable talking with you. They'll also be more inclined to contribute. Never underestimate the potential of anyone in the group. A compassionate leader does not deliberately try to make others feel that their contributions or opinions are insignificant. You don't want someone to begin feeling that he or she is invisible and consistently overlooked. Just imagine if every time you brought up an idea or recommendation, you were told it wasn't a good idea, or asked why we would do that, or informed that we were *not* going to do that. I've seen employees shut down because of such insulting behavior. The result: The leader loses.

Choose your words wisely. Think before you speak. Harsh words can have lasting and harmful effects. Mother Teresa said, "Kind words can be short and easy to speak, but their echoes are endless." Maintain professionalism in all situations. Never address anyone in a confrontational or condescending manner or engage in an argument. Words can destroy relationships. Practice saying positive things about people. It's incredibly unprofessional to mock, laugh at, or make fun of others.

Nonverbal communication can be as damaging as harsh words can be. Body language and facial expressions send visual messages and can create the same emotions and reactions that verbal communication can. I'm sure you've heard the phrase, "Actions speak louder than words." A pleasant look and a smile can be perceived as friendliness, approval or admiration.

Imagine this scenario: You're making a presentation in front of a small group of colleagues. Everyone has a smile and look of approval — except your supervisor. He has a slight frown and a disapproving stare. Another person makes a presentation after you and this time everyone, *including* the supervisor, has a smile and look of approval. After the meeting, everyone *but* the supervisor compliments you. You overhear him complimenting the other person, yet you receive no feedback. The supervisor's nonverbal communication during the presentation, whether intentional or unintentional, has the power to cause feelings of doubt, inadequacy and resentment.

Other negative, nonverbal communication includes whispering to one staff member in the presence of others, turning your back to one member in the group while speaking, avoiding eye contact, stepping in front of someone to cut them off from a conversation, rolling your eyes, and folding your arms tightly during a discussion. A compassionate leader would never function in this manner because of the negative impact these behaviors can have on another human being.

It's essential to be consciously aware of your body language and facial expressions. Learn the language of nonverbal communication to avoid sending negative messages. Choose your body language as carefully as you choose your words.

As Maya Angelou so eloquently stated, "I've learned that people will forget what you said, people will forget what you did, but people will never forget how you made them feel." How do you want to be remembered?

Avoid actions that hurt others. Every day, say something positive that makes someone feel good. Be compassionate.

Employee Welfare

"Injustice, prejudice and unfair treatment cannot be allowed to exist anywhere in the workplace."

~Dr. LaVerne Harmon

Employee Welfare

Concern for your employees' welfare is one of the most important responsibilities of the compassionate leader. People are your most valuable resources, yet they're sometimes overlooked. If you have managers and supervisors reporting to you, it's important to pay attention to their behaviors toward and treatment of subordinates. Don't trust or rely completely on their leadership abilities. Take a closer look at the ones who are experiencing conflict and controversy. Look for qualities of compassion and concern. Do they respect differences? Are they polite and respectful? Have they gained your trust? If the answer is no to any of these questions, he or she is not a compassionate leader. Consider implementing leadership training and requiring all current and future leaders to attend.

Evaluating managers and supervisors could be useful in identifying inappropriate actions. They should be held accountable for their behaviors, especially toward their subordinates. Of course, evaluation tools are rated subjectively, but if there's a common thread in the assessment results, it warrants a closer look. Perhaps the first follow-up could be a roundtable; an open discussion between the supervisor and department members to clarify responses that rendered low ratings. Participants must present concerns in non-threatening and non-judgmental ways, but that will only work if all parties are honest, open to constructive criticism, and present a sincere desire to improve.

Leaders should consistently practice equity and fairness and never show favoritism. Commit to promoting and encouraging a respect for diversity. Injustice, prejudice and unfair treatment cannot be allowed to exist anywhere in the workplace. We spend one-third of our lives working. I don't believe anyone enjoys spending that time in a work environment that's unpleasant and filled with unnecessary stress that's caused by poor leadership.

Compassionate leaders keep the welfare of employees in mind when developing policies that impact their work lives.

Attitude

"Attitude is a little thing that makes a big difference."

~Winston Churchill

Attitude

Attitude is important in leadership and in life. It reflects your character, your views, and the way you react to situations. A positive attitude promotes happiness and builds healthy, strong relationships. And you are the only one who can control your attitude.

A bad attitude can negatively impact your interactions and relationships. Leave your negative moods and problems at home, and don't take your frustrations out on others. Holding on to anger and resentment in the workplace interferes with building good relationships, reaching consensus and inspiring collaboration among your team and colleagues in other departments. You're only hurting yourself when you hold on to negative emotions, thus slowing down progress. Self-control is essential for effective leadership, so learn to manage your emotions. You cannot lead a team effectively until you've prepared yourself on an emotional level. The way you behave is your choice.

Compassionate leaders are aware of others' feelings and can maintain composure in tense situations. It's easier to address issues and conflict when you're levelheaded. If you have an anger management problem, you can seek counseling or consult self-help books. But first, you must a have a desire to change. If you don't, it will show in your words and actions.

Know your strengths and weaknesses, your inadequacies, and areas where you need more development, then actively seek ways to improve every aspect of your life. Misery loves company. If you're miserable, I guarantee it will adversely affect your leadership ability.

Integrity

"Let no pleasure tempt thee, no profit allure thee, no persuasion move thee to do anything which thou knowest to be evil."

~Benjamin Franklin

Integrity

Don't compromise your integrity. Have the courage to stand up for what is right. Be honest and forthright in all situations and never lie to cover up the truth. Evil plots against others will ultimately turn against you when the truth reveals itself. Promote someone based on his or her capabilities and good evaluations — not to spite someone else — because you could be setting someone up for failure. Reward and praise everyone for a job well done, but don't reward undeserving employees because you seek loyalty or some other return that benefits you. "The true measure of a man is how he treats someone who can do him absolutely no good," essayist Samuel Johnson said. In other words, don't give just to get something in return.

Cultivating good relationships is important. Get to know people. Spend time talking with them. Offer assistance when you can and make friends. If you're only kind to people or befriend someone when you need something, it won't be long before your modus operandi is exposed and your reputation tarnished. No one likes to be used.

Integrity is a significant component of your character. Let it resonate positively in everything you do. Disingenuous acts are callous. Avoid them at all costs.

Set Expectations

"A compassionate leader knows the importance of setting goals and monitoring progress and accomplishments, especially when it involves new or inexperienced employees."

~Dr. LaVerne Harmon

Set Expectations

For the compassionate leader, employee success should be the motivating factor when setting expectations. We give new hires their job descriptions, which list all the aspects and duties of the positions. The most important piece that's sometimes missing from the list are the goals, expectations and desired outcomes. A compassionate leader knows the importance of setting goals and monitoring progress, especially when it involves new or inexperienced employees. Goals should be shared with and understood by all involved parties. Good leaders set expectations early on and provide the necessary resources and guidance to accomplish tasks. Compassionate leaders also provide coaching and mentoring to encourage others to do their best.

Spend time with new employees to discuss the organization's culture. Explain the mission, goals and vision, and review the company history. Make new employees feel welcome by introducing them to other staff members, perhaps via a meet-and-greet social or one-on-one meeting. Recognize the contributions of current employees when presenting them to new hires.

For example, *I'd like you to meet Gayle, who has been with us for five years. During those five years, Gayle's done a great job. She revised our employee handbook to ensure compliance with state and federal regulations.* This small recognition has the power to motivate Gayle to do more and to encourage new employees to find ways to make an impact in the organization.

Compassionate leaders take time to get to know their employees. They're genuinely interested in them and want others to know that their work hasn't gone unnoticed.

Final Comments

"A true leader has the confidence to stand alone, the courage to make tough decisions, and the compassion to listen to the needs of others. He does not set out to be a leader, but becomes one by the equality of his actions and the integrity of his intent."

~Douglas MacArthur

Final Comments

I have attempted to provoke thought about what I feel is behind what we do and say. To me, it's the heart. Of course, I would never suggest that having compassion will make everything in your life conflict-free. That's unrealistic. But compassion will help you confront and manage difficult situations with a caring heart, and that can lessen frustration and stress.

You don't have to be abrasive or rule by intimidation to lead others or build a productive and loyal team. Compassionate leaders gain trust and support largely because of their caring and trusting nature. They're authentic and it shows. Remember, as a leader, you are the example. Others are watching your actions and interactions. If you display compassion, they will believe in you and want to copy your style. What example do you want to set?

If you're in a leadership position, I'm sure you've encountered personnel issues and conflicts. Or, if you advance to a leadership position, you will undoubtedly be confronted with those trials. When such problems arise, try to view them as opportunities. Think of conflict as a chance to turn a negative situation into a positive one, and an opportunity for all involved parties, including you, to learn. Approach every decision and judgment with compassion; keeping everyone's best interests in mind. You will discover that when you lead this way, it will alleviate stress and anxiety that could cloud your judgment and interfere with your ability to make good decisions.

When you incorporate compassion into your leadership style, you'll notice the difference it makes in your life and the lives of others. You will enjoy the emotions your good deeds create. Take the high road. If you don't, it's easy to take a wrong turn.

Enjoy your life and take it a day at a time. Make a commitment to contribute in as many ways as possible to improving the lives of those who cross you path. Valuing service above self is one of the greatest attributes any leader can possess.

At the end of each day ask yourself: What have I done today to help someone? Don't forget to meditate, pray and give thanks for making it through another day. Knowing that you live life as a compassionate person will help you sleep peacefully.

I share with you one of my favorite poems:

I Shall Not Live in Vain

by Emily Dickinson

If I can stop one heart from breaking,
I shall not live in vain;
If I can ease one life the aching,
Or cool one pain,
Or help one fainting robin
Unto his nest again,
I shall not live in vain.

Scenarios, Analysis and Lessons

The following fictional scenarios were developed to help you contemplate the importance of compassion and what can occur without it.

In this section, I have developed fictional workplace scenarios that illustrate how one supervisor's mistake led to several personnel issues — and how a leader who lacked compassion created a toxic environment. Following the scenarios, I offer analysis and lessons for compassionate leaders that I hope you'll find helpful.

Implementing a New Policy

An organization's administrative team, which consisted of the president and vice presidents, met to discuss a proposed policy change. There was a lot of disagreement during the meeting until the group finally came to a consensus. Each member left the meeting with the understanding that they would stand unified in support of the revised policy. Supervisors were informed of the new policy and then asked by each vice president to convey to their subordinates the change in a positive manner.

Mr. Ruthers, a supervisor, was adamantly opposed to the change. He did not express his feelings to Dr. Silvers, a vice president. He presented the change to his staff in a negative way. As a result of this supervisor's reaction, no one in his department was receptive to the policy change.

Analysis

Ruthers's first mistake was not supporting the administration. He should have voiced his opinion and concerns to the vice president, who could have offered more information to justify the change. Ruthers can be charged with insubordination since his actions were against the vice president's directives. Secondly, he should never have shared with the staff his opposing views of the policy change.

Lessons for the compassionate leader

- Ignoring directives could lead to charges of insubordination.
- Support change in a positive manner to create unity and support.
- Don't share your opposition with subordinates to garner support for your point of view. It creates a division among employees.

Communication

Ruthers does not hold regular staff meetings and is sometimes too flexible and laid back. Samantha, one of the eight staff members who report to him, is the only one who receives constant praise and acknowledgement for her accomplishments. It so happens that Ruthers has developed a friendly working and social relationship with Samantha.

Analysis

There are several issues going on here. Communication is stagnant due to the lack of regular staff meetings. It questions whether Ruthers is fully informed of what's going on within the department.

He's making a terrible mistake by not acknowledging the accomplishments of all staff members. Also, the relationship he has developed with one employee is putting him in a compromising situation.

Lessons for the compassionate leader

- Leaders shouldn't be too friendly, too flexible, or too laid back with their subordinates. They have to know where to draw the line.
- Regular staff meetings are necessary to keep the lines of communication open.
- When you allow yourself to become one of the gang, you risk losing respect. You have to set yourself apart from your staff and maintain a professional relationship.

Staff Relations

Staff members are jealous of Ruthers's and Samantha's relationship and begin spreading rumors. There's a lot of gossip and discussion going on when they're not around.

Analysis

Now you see the results of Ruthers's mistakes and the effects they can have on staff. Favoritism towards Samantha has created jealousy and resentment. Issues of inequity can create disloyalty among staff and generate poor morale — not to mention a lack of respect for the supervisor.

Lessons for the compassionate leader

- Avoid spending time alone with subordinates whether on- or off-site. It could create speculation and gossip about the relationship. It also creates jealousy and resentment among staff members.
- Treat employees equally to avoid accusations of favoritism and unfairness — and to maintain your subordinates' respect.

Boundaries and Chain of Command

During a discussion among staff members, Samantha said that since Ruthers didn't fight against the policy change, she intended to meet with Silvers to express her dissatisfaction. She wanted an explanation for the change. Samantha believed that by meeting with the vice president, she would be able to help her supervisor get his point across and explain his opposition.

Analysis

The relationship Ruthers created with Samantha gave this employee a sense of power to say and do whatever she wanted without concern for her actions.

Lessons for the compassionate leader

- Maintain a professional relationship with subordinates so that boundaries are clear.
- Make sure employees understand the chain of command and are informed that concerns should be addressed *first* with their immediate supervisors.

Speculation, Accusations, Gossip

Jason, one of the staff members, told Ruthers that Samantha planned to meet with Vice President Silvers to voice a complaint about the new policy. Ruthers's immediate reaction was anger. He assumed that because Samantha didn't discuss this with him, she was going to report that he wasn't supportive of the policy change. Ruthers then developed feelings of distrust and began questioning Samantha's motives — someone he believed to be loyal.

Jason saw how upset Ruthers was and asked to be anonymous. He then proceeded to exaggerate the truth, hoping to ruin the relationship between Ruthers and Samantha. Jason didn't explain that Samantha wanted to speak with Silvers to gain support for Ruthers's opposition to the policy.

Analysis

This case is getting more complex. Ruthers is speculating quite a bit. He has also jumped to conclusions about Samantha, making accusations without communicating with her. If he had, he might have understood her intent for the meeting request. Samantha wasn't even aware that her actions were inappropriate.

In addition, Jason's motives stem from his jealousy of Ruthers's and Samantha's relationship. So when Ruthers agreed to Jason's anonymity, he opened the door for Jason to stretch the truth.

Lessons for the compassionate leader

- Don't speculate.
- Get the facts before reacting to information brought to you. Talk with those accused.
- Communicate with all parties involved before drawing conclusions.

Intimidation

Ruthers met with Samantha to discuss the information he received from Jason. In an angry and loud tone, he threatened Samantha, telling her that if she went over his head and outside the department to complain, there would be consequences, possibly even termination. Although she tried, Samantha wasn't allowed to defend herself and Ruthers didn't reveal his source. She left the meeting regretting that she had created such a fiasco. She decided to drop the issue, choosing not to meet with Silvers. Samantha didn't realize the problem it would cause for Ruthers, and wished she had been given the opportunity to explain.

Analysis

Ruthers continues to exhibit a lack of judgment and make erroneous leadership decisions. He had thought initially that verbal attacks and intimidation were the only ways to gain control. He didn't take time to learn the details or analyze the situation. Instead, he drew conclusions based on gossip, speculation and assumptions, and reacted negatively to what he viewed as a personal attack. This created an environment of distrust and suspicion. He believed the gossip, and that weakened him.

Lessons for the compassionate leader

- Maintain composure in every situation by controlling your emotions.
- Lead with compassion and employees will follow you because they want to, not because they're intimidated. Start with discouraging gossip.
- Allow subordinates to voice their points of view, opinions and concerns. Truly listen to them.

Composure and Professionalism

The next day, Ruthers stopped all communication with Samantha and spoke to her only in passing. Samántha became suspicious and withdrawn. She never understood what she did wrong, so she felt helpless and abandoned.

Analysis

Ruthers created a hostile environment. His behavior caused anxiety, stress and paranoia.

Lessons for the compassionate leader

- You can't shut down communication, especially when there's a situation that hasn't been resolved. So resolve it completely.
- Regardless of the situation, leaders must remain professional at all times. You are setting an example.

Poor Judgment and Bad Decisions

Employee evaluations are due a week after all this drama has taken place. Samantha is the only staff member who received her performance review in the interoffice mail, along with a note from Ruthers to sign and return. She's concerned that she wasn't scheduled for the usual one-on-one evaluation. Plus, she received low ratings in several areas in which she had been previously and consistently rated as exceptional.

Analysis

Ruthers continues to make bad decisions. His issues with anger management and self-control have caused this case to become unmanageable. His emotional instability and lack of compassion have interfered with his ability to lead fairly.

Lessons for the compassionate leader

- Good decisions are based on fact, not speculation. Don't let your emotions control challenging situations. No matter how upset you may be, try to think clearly, even if you have to escape for a few hours to regroup.
- Communication should remain open regardless of the situation.
- Lead with equity and fairness. Every employee and colleague matters, and it's up to you to make them feel that way.

Lack of Compassion and Personnel Issues

The situation has escalated. After seeing no resolution, Samantha schedules a meeting with the vice president. She feels she has no other choice but to defend herself.

Analysis

What a waste of time, energy and resources! The relationship between Samantha and Ruthers appears irreparable. This case has developed into a personnel issue that will require resolution at a higher level.

Lessons for the compassionate leader

- Bad decisions, speculation and poor judgment can be costly. Had the supervisor led with compassion, this situation could have been prevented or at least minimized.

Reflection Worksheet

Reflection Worksheet

Now that you've read the book and case scenarios, I invite you to reflect on the following questions.

- As a subordinate, have you worked in an environment where your supervisor lacked compassion?

____

____

____

____

____

____

- Describe a specific situation in which he or she lacked compassion.

____

____

____

____

____

____

- What were some of the behaviors he or she displayed?

____
____
____
____
____
____

- Were you affected by those behaviors? If yes, how did it feel?

____
____
____
____
____
____

- Name the manager's specific behaviors that you would not want to emulate.

____
____
____
____
____
____

Now answer the following questions with the previous reflections in mind. Be honest. This is for your benefit.

- What is your understanding of compassion?

____

____

____

____

____

____

- In terms of being compassionate, how would you rate yourself on a scale from one to 1 to 10, with 10 being the highest?

  1 2 3 4 5 6 7 8 9 10

- Are you aware of mistakes you've made in your treatment of others? If so, list those mistakes.

____

____

____

____

____

____

- What would you do differently now that you are more aware of the importance of compassion?

____

____

____

____

____

____

- What specific behaviors should you develop to become more compassionate?

____

____

____

____

____

____

Suggestions

With your reflections in mind, consider utilizing the following ideas:

Keep a journal of situations and interactions that lack compassion. List ways that detail how those situations could be improved. Be aware of the needs of others around you. What are you noticing now that you didn't notice before? Add that to your journal.

Now that you've reflected honestly, rethink our case scenarios.

- Should Vice President Silvers schedule an appointment with Samantha?

  ____

  ____

  ____

  ____

  ____

  ____

- Should Silvers contact Ruthers first to discern why Samantha wants to meet with him?

____

____

____

____

____

____

- How would you proceed?

____

____

____

____

____

____

- What value will compassion add to your decision?

____

____

____

____

____

____

One More Note

I hope your reflections have helped you consider what compassionate leadership is, and how you can incorporate a new kind of thinking into your leadership role. Remember, compassion is not a weakness; it's a strength.

This book is from my heart to yours. I wish you well.

"May you be rooted and grounded in love."

Ephesians 3:17

Acknowledgements

This has been the most difficult section of the book to write. I guess you're wondering why. Well, there are so many individuals and situations — starting with my childhood—from which I've learned. My parents, husband, siblings, teachers, supervisors, colleagues and many others have provided valuable life lessons. I wish I could list every one of you by name, but if I did, this book might never end! Thank you all, from the bottom of my heart.

I have vivid memories of things that made me happy and others that were hurtful. I'm thankful for all of those experiences because they made me aware of the impact my actions have on others. I remind you of Emily Dickinson's poignant words: *If I can stop one heart from breaking, I shall not live in vain.*

I sincerely thank those who were committed to helping me publish this book. They were heaven-sent.

Finally, I'm deeply grateful to God for the wisdom, understanding and knowledge to write, "The Heart of Leadership." I am truly blessed.

"To lead is to love and to love is to lead."

~Thais K. Greca (my niece)

About the Author

Dr. LaVerne Harmon is president of Wilmington University and the first African-American woman to be named the president of a college or university in the state of Delaware. She holds a doctorate in Higher Education Administration from the University of Pennsylvania.

Dr. Harmon joined the staff of Wilmington University (then college) in 1989 and held numerous positions while earning undergraduate and graduate degrees from Wilmington University. Like many of the university's students, she worked full-time for 10 consecutive years while earning all three degrees. As her career progressed, she held key roles in the university's internal operations, planning and strategic growth, and her collaborative leadership style and diverse experiences prepared her for the expanding role of university president.

Dr. Harmon has earned myriad awards and served on numerous nonprofit boards. She is an ardent proponent of community service.

Notes

Notes

Made in the USA
Coppell, TX
04 February 2020